A DUSTY DIAMOND

Exchanging Darkness for Light through Forgiveness

Mary Call Munger

WESTBOW°
PRESS
A DIVISION OF THOMAS NELSON
& ZONDERVAN

Scripture taken from the Holy Bible, NEW INTERNATIONAL VERSION®. Copyright © 1973, 1978, 1984 by Biblica, Inc. All rights reserved worldwide. Used by permission. NEW INTERNATIONAL VERSION® and NIV® are registered trademarks of Biblica, Inc. Use of either trademark for the offering of goods or services requires the prior written consent of Biblica US, Inc.

All Scripture quotations in this publications are from The Message. Copyright © by Eugene H. Peterson 1993, 1994, 1995, 1996, 2000, 2001, 2002. Used by permission of NavPress Publishing Group.

Scripture taken from the *Amplified Bible*, copyright © 1954, 1958, 1962, 1964, 1965, 1987 by The Lockman Foundation. Used by permission.

Scripture taken from the King James Version of the Bible.

Good News Translation® (Today's English Version, Second Edition) Copyright © 1992 American Bible Society. All rights reserved.

Scripture quotations taken from the Holy Bible, New Living Translation, Copyright © 1996, 2004. Used by permission of Tyndale House Publishers, Inc., Wheaton, Illinois 60189. All rights reserved.

WestBow Press books may be ordered through booksellers or by contacting:

WestBow Press
A Division of Thomas Nelson & Zondervan
1663 Liberty Drive
Bloomington, IN 47403
www.westbowpress.com
1 (866) 928-1240

Because of the dynamic nature of the Internet, any web addresses or links contained in this book may have changed since publication and may no longer be valid. The views expressed in this work are solely those of the author and do not necessarily reflect the views of the publisher, and the publisher hereby disclaims any responsibility for them.

Any people depicted in stock imagery provided by Thinkstock are models, and such images are being used for illustrative purposes only. Certain stock imagery © Thinkstock.

ISBN: 978-1-4908-8136-2 (sc)
ISBN: 978-1-4908-8135-5 (e)

Library of Congress Control Number: 2015908055

Print information available on the last page.

WestBow Press rev. date: 05/22/2015

Contents

Honors Page

I would like to take this opportunity to honor the dear Christian brothers and sisters all around the globe; who are suffering and persecuted for the sake of the gospel. As an American born citizen it is difficult to imagine the pain and misery endured by these humble Christians in other parts of the world. Some face imprisonment, torture, isolation, dismemberment, family abandonment, slavery, and all kinds of other intimidation that I can't even conceive. These beloved Christian men and women are united with us as members of the family of Christ. We should count it an honor and blessing to pray for these precious Christians who are suffering and being persecuted.

> *"Keep on loving each other as brothers. 3) Remember those in prison as if you were their fellow prisoners, and those who are mistreated as if you yourselves were suffering." Hebrews 13:1 and 3 NIV*

In honor of Pastor J. Rebecca Tate, the former pastor of Grace Pentecostal Holiness Church, for your teaching and leadership.

In honor of Pastor Mark Ivey, of Christ Alive Church, for accepting Ray and me into the congregation you are leading.

Dedication

For family, friends and anyone who reads this work.

"It is for freedom that Christ has set us free. Stand firm, then, and do not let yourselves be burdened again by a yoke of slavery. Galatians 5:1 NIV

Acknowledgments

Thank you to friends and family for encouragement
and support

Rita, Alice, Tom and Tim

"But everything exposed by the light becomes visible—and everything that is illuminated becomes a light." Ephesians 5:13 NIV

CHAPTER 1

A Dusty Diamond

> *"For God, who said, "Let light shine out of darkness,"
> made his light shine in our hearts to give us the
> light of the knowledge of God's glory displayed in
> the face of Christ." 2 Corinthians 4:6 NIV*

The struggle with our painful past is like a piece of coal residing in our inner most being. That chunk of coal is black and hard and produces no light. When we accept the truth that Jesus Christ is the son of God, and receive His forgiveness at that very moment God replaces that blackness in our souls with the light of truth. That light of truth is contained in what I am referring to as a Dusty Diamond. This diamond is an image of the perfect light showing that Jesus is living inside our hearts. Just imagine the facets of a beautiful polished diamond. As we turn it over in our hand we can see the brilliance of its inner beauty and light. The top is smooth and so clear we can see down to the point. It is no wonder that the world seeks after this beautiful gem. Now imagine that same jewel with dark marks all over the facets, just as if a black marker was used to try and cover the light shining from its center. As we look at this diamond so defaced we can get a mental picture of how sin and past regrets can cover the surface of our diamond making it dusty and hard for the light to shine through. The cut facets of this precious jewel which is our innermost being contain the life events that have carved their way onto the surface. The hurts and cares of our history blanket each side with another layer of dust until this diamond who is the real person we are in Christ becomes almost unrecognizable. All the memories of sin and pain in our past layer that diamond with dust which needs to be removed to allow the light to shine forth.

> *"Instruct the wise and they will be wiser still; teach the righteous and they will add to their learning."*
> **Proverbs 9:9 NIV**

The subject of this study began several years ago while I was leading a small group of new believers at church. The class consisted of about a dozen people, all at different places in their recent conversion to Christianity. Men and women alike had many questions about living a Christian life. The focus began to turn to how to survive with past hurts and sins and still live a life pleasing to God. One of the younger ladies kept asking about all the pain she had experienced in her childhood. The remembrance of the pain she had suffered was causing her to withdraw from the truth. As I was attempting to reassure her, the Lord shared with me the answer that not only helped her understand, but also brought about the subject of this study.

I am a visual learner. So when the Lord revealed to me that our lives are like the facets of a cut diamond, my understanding of the hurting soul truly expanded. The coal from which a raw diamond is made is under great tons of pressure for many years. Our lives before Christ are like that chunk of coal. We sometimes go through so many trials and pressure that a deep darkness develops around our souls. It seems that this heaviness will not produce anything but a constant reoccurring heartache. At these times when the tension seems overwhelming, we can't focus on what good might come out of these painful past trials. Still just knowing that the Lord forgave and accepted us with all our troubles brings us more peace than we have ever known before. But even with that truth we are just like that raw diamond still under pressure. When the time is right and the tons of pressure have done their job, the miner can take the raw diamond from the dirt. Now the jeweler can examine the stone closely for faults. In order for the value of the gem to be revealed, he chips away at the rough edges and polishes until the facets begin to show. Only after hours or days of this work to remove those raw edges does the diamond begin to show forth its beauty and value. There are countless facets that reveal the splendor of the cut stone. But without the jeweler's knowledge and work the gemstone would just be another rock.

> *"For the Word that God speaks is alive and full of power [making it active, operative, energizing, and effective]; it is sharper than any two-edged sword, penetrating to the dividing line of the breath of life (soul) and [the immortal] spirit, and of joints and marrow [of the deepest parts of our nature], exposing and sifting and analyzing and judging the very thoughts and purposes of the heart." Hebrews 4:12 AMP*

Surely it takes time and skill to reveal the value of the raw diamond. The unveiling of the polished stone of our hearts can also be time consuming and uncomfortable. But in order for the light of Jesus to shine from our Dusty Diamond we must allow the Lord to remove those raw and painful memories. Once we surrender our lives and begin to respond to the Lord and to the study of the Word of God, the truth that is alive and powerful will begin to chip away and polish those rough edges until the facets of our lives begin to reveal the light of Jesus. But as we continually rerun in our minds those hurtful memories we take our focus off Jesus and hinder our growth and progress in Christ. As this happens the dust slowly begins to build more layers around the jewel of our heart. Yet that diamond still contains within its center the light that comes from Jesus Christ alone which will cause the changes necessary to bring about victory and peace in our lives.

> *"Give thanks to the LORD, for he is good; his love endures forever.² Let the redeemed of the LORD tell their story— those he redeemed from the hand of the foe," Psalm 107:1-2 NIV*

My past was so full of pain and mistakes I never imagined it possible that God would place that diamond inside of me. As a teen and young adult I was very antisocial and angry at the world. Those were dark and miserable days with no real answers except what I could conceive on my own. There was no reason for real joy because the daily abuse had taken over my existence. Deciding at a very young age to not allow my spirit to be broken, I began to withdraw from the hurt by looking inward. But my insides were as dark as the pain surrounding my life. Even sleep was not an escape. There was this recurring childhood nightmare where I was being chased down a dark tunnel by a figure in black. At the end of the tunnel was a bright light, but I could never reach it, and would awake in a panic. Only after I accepted Jesus in my life did this troublesome dream stop. Then God replaced that darkness with the diamond that contains the light of Jesus and Jesus sent the Holy Spirit. Do I have all the answers? No, but God does, and life is much better now that the Word of God has allowed me to see that bitterness solves nothing. Resentment only brings me down, not the people who caused the harm in my past. By giving these circumstances over to the Lord He has shown me the only answer to these bad memories and dreams is to accept Jesus and forgive others.

> *"You, dear children, are from God and have overcome them, because the <u>one who is in you is greater than the one who is in the world.</u> 5) They*

are from the world and therefore speak from the viewpoint of the world, and the world listens to them. ⁶⁾ We are from God, and whoever knows God listens to us; but whoever is not from God does not listen to us. This is how we recognize the Spirit of truth and the spirit of falsehood." 1 John 4:4-6 NIV

The Dusty Diamond that is central to our lives as a Christian is waiting to shine the light of Jesus to the world. The light may be very small at first, because of all the dust from bad memories that quickly covers the surface of our diamond. Even so a single match can show forth light in a dark area. As we forgive the dust is being removed from our diamond and the light of Jesus inside our diamond shines brighter. This in turn causes people to be either drawn to us or repelled by the light. I have had people surprise me by apologizing for using profane language in my presence. These people are somehow sensitive to the light and are therefore aware of what they are saying and how their words may offend others. Even though they may not be a Christian they recognize the light and can show respect for others. Still I hear other people talk vulgar in front of everyone including myself without any regard for even the age or gender of the people that could hear their words. These people who are full of darkness show they are blind to the light and do not care that what they are saying may be offensive to anyone else. This disregard and disrespect for other people may be their way of resisting the light they don't understand. Yet I have not said to either group that I am a Christian. In fact I had an unsaved co-worker say "If you have to tell me you are a Christian then I doubt you are." She said this because a woman we worked with would tell everyone she was a Christian, but her actions did not show that she had a true relationship with the Lord, or a love for others. She would daily complain about the working conditions and tried to correct everyone's mistakes. This in turn would cause those who worked with her to question how a Christian was supposed to act.

Her statement made an impression on me because I agree with what she said. People tend to watch our walk instead of listen to our talk. Does this mean that we are to never tell people about our relationship with the Lord? Of course not! But remember people recall most often what you do and forget most of what you say. Let us live like that light is very important because Jesus is the light inside our Dusty Diamond.

Just like a diamond in the jeweler's hand have countless facets, so does our lives. Our focus at this time may be on the pain of the past but it doesn't have to stay there. Our attention can now be directed to God who has provided a way out of the troubles of our past. The mercy of the Lord is so great it can overtake and remove those memories that are attempting to hold us back. When God places the light of Christ, which is contained in the Dusty Diamond, in our lives we not only have the hope of heaven but we can begin to live with hope for today and tomorrow.

A Dusty Diamond Q&A:

#1.When was the diamond placed inside our hearts?

_____

_____

2 Corinthians 4:6 NIV

#2. Who can help us handle the problems in our past?

_____

_____

Romans 12:17-19 MSG

#3. What is in us that is greater than what the world offers?

_____

_____

1 John 4:4-6 NIV

#4. Should we testify about what God has done for us?

_____

_____

Psalm 107:1-2 NIV

#5. How can the dust be removed from the diamond of our hearts?

_____

_____

Hebrews 4:12 AMP

For God so greatly loved and dearly prized the world that He [even] gave up His only begotten (unique) Son, so that whoever believes in (trusts in, clings to, relies on) Him shall not perish (come to destruction, be lost) but have eternal (everlasting) life. John 3:16 The Amplified Bible

CHAPTER 2

The Birth Condition

"Surely I was sinful at birth, sinful from the time my mother conceived me." Psalm 51:5 NIV

There is only one way we can receive that diamond that contains the light of Jesus. And there is a condition that stands in the way of the exchange we are seeking. According to the Bible we are all born with the same condition or principle of sin. Sin is the condition that causes us to be separated from the love and mercy of God. From the time of Adam's fall, we have all inherited the principle of sin in our inner most being. As babies we were born innocent, but eventually the sin principle breaks through and shows itself in behavior. This principle of sin we inherited at birth cannot be removed without the forgiveness offered by Jesus Christ.

"There's a way of life that looks harmless enough; look again – it leads to hell. Sure, those people appear to be having a good time, but all that laughter will end in heartbreak." Proverbs 14:12 The Message Bible

With all the world's cultural differences which include our varied skin color and gender we human beings all share the same biological composition. Scientists have proven in this age of DNA testing that we are all related. Even with a generational spread of centuries, this DNA can be traced back to a single pair of individuals. Because of this relationship to one another we all share the same condition of sin. That sin has been trying to keep us captive to the evil attempting to control our lives. Inside our minds and soul is a blackness that is working to convince us there is no way out causing us feel completely helpless to do anything about this torment. Because of this inner torment as sinners we are prone to do and say things that are selfish and hurtful. It is our very nature to be more concerned about our own wellbeing than that of the people around us. Certainly there are times when we are not totally selfish, and can honestly show concern for someone else. Still, even those acts of seemly unselfish conduct are not enough to remove the root of bitterness forming around our hearts. The schemes and plans we are working on to try and remove our selfish behavior will never bring about the results of peace that we truly seek. The failure of these awkward attempts to remove our inner bitterness can cause a downward path into deep depression. However the Holy Spirit and the Word of God will bring us the truth that will set us free and show us that Jesus is the answer to our sinful condition.

> *This righteousness from God comes through faith in Jesus Christ to all who believe. There is no difference 23) for all have sinned and fall short of the glory of God, 24) and are justified freely by His grace through redemption that came by Christ Jesus. Romans 3:22-24 NIV*

Sadly there are times we may go for years before we decide that enough is enough. Have you heard the phrase "If you keep doing what you have been doing, you will keep getting what you have been getting?" Are you sick and tired of the same old merry-go-round, always ending up in the same place, with the same type of people? I am a perfect example. In the past there were many times when I would move on to another person, another city, another job, just to end up where I started, with even more regretful memories, and heartaches. Looking to other people, places and things to change my circumstances did nothing to satisfy the longing for love and acceptance for which I was searching. Still somewhere deep inside my soul I knew there was an answer. The prayers offered up for me by my Grandmother Frances were being heard by the Lord. God was wooing me, but at that time I was too caught up in my pain and regret to know what to do about this sin problem. My excuse was like so many others I have heard; "I have sinned too much for God to love me." Only after years of pain and sorrow did I realize that I was totally powerless to solve this dilemma of sin. After much soul searching and coming to the end of myself did I find there was a way out of this sinful condition. God was offering me a much more productive way to take than the same old dark path of sinful behavior.

"Brothers, I do not consider myself yet to have taken hold of it. But one thing I do; forgetting what is behind and straining toward what is ahead, 14) I press on toward the goal to win the prize for which God has called me heavenward in Christ Jesus." Philippians 3:13-14 NIV

My personal history was full of scars from an abusive tormented past. Deep wounds caused ugly scars that were beyond my limited ability to remove. It was only when I accepted Jesus Christ as my Savior that God forgave me and sent the Holy Spirit. The Holy Spirit and the Word of God replaced those memories with the truth that God loves me regardless of what happened years ago. The pain from past events now has no power over my future. The light of Christ that began to reside in my soul yearned to break me free of the darkness and pain of abuse and distress. The more productive path became a reality for me only after I accepted Jesus as my Lord and Savior.

Although God has all we need and is willing to remove our pain, it is necessary to surrender our hearts and lives to Jesus Christ before the exchange can begin. The simple truth is if we are not a Christian with a true relationship with God the Father, Jesus Christ his son and the Holy Spirit, then the exchange of our torment for his life of peace is not possible. As the Apostle Paul said in Romans 10:9-10

> *"That if you confess with your mouth, "Jesus is Lord", and believe in your heart that God raised him from the dead, you will be saved. 10) For it is with your heart that you believe and are justified, and it is with your mouth that you confess and are saved." Romans 10:9-10 NIV*

If your desire is to surrender your heart and life to Jesus, then repent from the sinful ways you have been living. To repent means to turn away from the sin that separates you from God. Then simply accept what Jesus did for you on the cross. Jesus took your sin as He died. He took those sins to the grave. Then He rose again leaving your sins behind. Jesus was seen after his resurrection by His disciples and many others. He was taken up to heaven before them, and now sits at the right hand of God the Father, making intercession on your behalf. The prayer offered in faith will be heard by God the Father. God will forgive those sins you confessed and place within you the diamond that contains the light of Jesus. It doesn't matter where you are or where you have been. There is no sin so great that God won't forgive. If you said that prayer and meant it from your heart, God has placed that diamond that contains the light of Jesus within your innermost being, and Jesus has given you the Holy Spirit. With the assistance of the Holy Spirit and the Word of God there are possibilities of a new and better life full of promise. However even after entering into this new life with Christ we still have the same body and the same memories of the past. Those dark memories from our past will begin to cover that diamond with the dust that dims its light. Still there is no reason to lose hope. The Holy Spirit was sent by Jesus to be our helper and guide. He will help us understand that there needs to be a change from past routines and bad habits.

Without the Holy Spirit's leading and obedience to the Word of God we would continue in the sinful condition that brought us to the cross in the first place. We must realize that the blood of Jesus has washed away our sin. We need the Holy Spirit and God's Word to direct us into how to live the Christian life. How could we possibly know the difference? We have come out of a dark sinful existence into the light of the truth. The Lord will provide all we need for life but we still need to study the Bible to learn His ways. Obedience to the Word of God will enable us to repent and replace those sinful habits with behaviors that will produce in us the desire to serve the Lord and the people around us.

In order to make sense of these sudden new changes in our lives the Bible will become the written Word that we need to study. Make an effort to set aside time every day to read the Bible and pray. To pray means just having a conversation with God. As our lives develop in Christ according to the Word of God we learn more and more about how to pray. God will always respond to our willingness to the study of the Bible and prayer. God is always listening and desires to answer our prayers. Consider attending a Bible believing church and maybe joining a small group study with other believers. It is much easier to grow in the Lord with the support and prayers of likeminded people. I found it most helpful to listen to encouraging Christian music. There is a style on the radio for every variety available from gospel hymns to Christian rock. The World Wide Web has many teachers and resources available for purchase or download. There are also Christian books, TV stations and countless movies on DVD or Blu-ray. So whatever is needed to help us grow as a Christian is available in whatever form we are comfortable with. Take advantage of all the resources accessible to each person. There are big changes ahead. Hold on to the promises from the Lord and never let go, because God is with us in a new way.

Now that we are on the same level field at the foot of the cross we can begin to understand what role the Holy Spirit and the Word of God has in our future. For without the ministering of the Holy Spirit and instruction from the Word of God we will not know the truth from a lie. Even though we did inherit a principle of sin at birth, we no longer have to live under that dark cloud. Jesus Christ is the only way out of that dilemma of sin. So trust in and accept Jesus and allow God to replace that darkness of the past with the diamond that contains the light of Jesus. Then the Holy Spirit can assist us to forgive which will show forth the light of Jesus from our Dusty Diamond.

My desire is to show the reader that the Holy Spirit and the Word of God will enable each of us to live a more tranquil and productive life. That is the function of the Holy Spirit and the Word of God in our lives. Working together they take the pain and hurt of the past and exchange it for the healing power of Jesus Christ. The damage from past hurts can be repaired with the mercy and grace offered by the Lord. God has given us the Holy Spirit and His Word to guide us into that state of forgiveness that will bring about healing. The Holy Spirit when allowed by us will exchange the hurt, pain and darkness for healing, recovery and strength that is promised to us in the Bible. An act of forgiveness can start the cleansing process. As this cleansing begins it will bring out the sparkle in our Dusty Diamond.

The Birth Condition Q&A:

#1.What condition is common to all human beings?

_____

_____

Psalm 51:5 NIV

#2. Who has the answer to our sin problem?

_____

_____

Romans 6:11-13 NIV

#3. What causes the diamond in our soul to become dusty?

_____

_____

#4. How are we to receive salvation?

_____

_____

Romans 10:9-13 NIV

#5. How can you learn how to live a Christian life?

_____

_____

#6. Are you ready to surrender your life to the Lord?

_____

_____

John 3:16 NIV

#7. What changes did you experience when you received salvation?

_____

_____

If we confess our sins, he is faithful and just and will forgive us our sins and purify us from all unrighteousness. 10) If we claim we have not sinned, we make him out to be a liar and his word has no place in our lives. 1 John 1 9-10 NIV

CHAPTER 3

Forgiveness

> *"Be sure of this: The wicked will not go unpunished,*
> *but those who are righteous will go free." Proverbs*
> *11:21 NIV*

If there is one vital key to releasing the light of Jesus in our Dusty Diamond it is the act of forgiveness. Forgiveness releases the heart from hurts, the mind from anger, and the body from stress. Forgiveness opens the way for the work of the Holy Spirit and the Word of God. Even with such spiritual benefits however, we often still continue to hold on to the pain of the past. It is not unusual to want the pain that was perpetrated on us to be returned with interest on the people responsible. Because of this history of troubles we have:

* A heart with hurts that can't love.
* A mind full of anger that searches for peace.
* A body reacting to stress that can't get relief or healing.
* A guilty soul that will not experience freedom.

The hurts and memories from the past of what was done to us haunt our minds and builds a layer of bitterness around our hearts. Forgiveness can be extremely difficult. But to allow love, joy, and peace to take place in our life, forgiveness is a necessity. Now that we have been released from the principle of sin by accepting the forgiveness God offers through Jesus Christ, we need to learn how to extend that same forgiveness to others. Forgiveness is the desire to release the burden of bitterness toward someone and to give them completely over to God. It is the memories of the past that are consuming our minds and standing in the way of progress. To move forward we must release those memories, and the people who caused those painful memories, and give them over to the Lord. In order for us to experience a fulfilled successful life as a Christian we must learn to forgive.

Some individuals are so filled with dark memories that they seem to be only happy with a pity party instead of a peace pipe. But most of us want freedom from those dark past hurts instead of pity. There needs to be a submission to the idea that we can never relive the events of the past and be able to change what happened at that time. You ask;" What about my trial? You have no idea what I have been through! You are asking me to forgive that?!? There must be some other way!!" I understand more than you know how extremely difficult it can be, but Jesus said it best in Matthew 6:14-15 NIV

> *"For if you forgive men when they sin against you, your heavenly Father will also forgive you 15) But if you do not forgive men their sins, your Father will not forgive your sins." Matthew 6: 14-15 NIV*

Forgiveness is a major tool the Holy Spirit uses to bring about the exchange of stress to rest that we desire. As we begin to see what God's Word is teaching us about the release we will gain through forgiveness, we start to understand how important it is for us to forgive. Forgiveness will cause our heart to stop aching. It brings our body into a calmer state, and takes away the feeling of guilt that is trying to rob us of our freedom. But if we refuse to forgive we are only hurting ourselves and cutting off the ability for God to move on our behalf. Certainly when we received salvation God forgave our sins and therefore we are going to heaven. However we find in the scriptures that if we do not forgive others we lose God's blessing in that area of our lives. Thankfully the Lord is always available to support us in the process of forgiving, although there may be many tears wept before we can experience the exchange from turmoil to peace. The bitterness that has been building up for a long time could take an extended period of time to loosen its grip on our hearts. We are seeking the exchange that comes from Christ through obedience to the Word of God and the act of forgiveness. When we begin to understand that forgiveness starts the healing process for us then we will desire to quickly forgive others. In doing so we not only receive forgiveness but we can grant forgiveness. God is willing to forgive us all our sins but we must be obedient to His Word and be willing to learn to forgive others.

> *"Do not repay anyone evil for evil. Be careful to do what is right in the eyes of everybody. 18) If it is possible, as far as it depends on you, live at peace with everyone. Romans 12:17-18 NIV*

Forgiveness from us is only possible with the assistance of the Holy Spirit and obedience to the Word of God. We may struggle with the idea of forgiveness because it is a completely new concept we have not considered before. God understands that we can have a real struggle in learning to forgive. If we desire revenge, to repay evil with evil, then we are not practicing forgiveness. Our record of wrongs will never solve the problem we are having with our past. We must first trust that God is on our side and will handle those circumstances in His perfect timing. Our minds will argue that we just allowed the people that hurt us to get away free and clear. But this lie will keep us from receiving the blessing of release God desires we experience. The truth is no one ever gets away with anything. The only positive way to exchange your turmoil for peace is to forgive and release all those bad memories over to the Lord. God is just and will avenge the pain we suffered at the hands of sinful individuals. Our desiring revenge is not the answer, the only answer is forgiveness.

> *"Do not take revenge, my friends, but leave room for God's wrath, for it is written: "It is mine to avenge; I will repay," says the Lord.20) On the contrary: "If your enemy is hungry, feed him; if he is thirsty, give him something to drink. In doing this, you will heap burning coals on his head." 21) Do not be overcome by evil, but overcome evil with good." Romans 12:19-21 NIV*

Forgiveness can be as simple or as complicated as is needed to deal with the memories of the past. Some hurtful issues may be easy to forgive. While others may take a long time to get freedom from the bitterness that has built up in our souls. So what are the steps we should take to forgive someone?

*First we need to release our desire for vengeance. By releasing our desire for vengeance we allow the Holy Spirit to replace those hurt feelings with the assurance that God is truly on our side. This will allow us to focus our energy on forgiving instead of getting even.

**Secondly we need to understand that God is in charge of judging sin and He is faithful. Will you see the perpetrators punished for their crimes against you? The fact is if we desire or demand to witness their punishment then we have not fully forgiven them, nor do we understand that God is in charge of all justice. Holding on to the resentment will withhold God's hand from their punishment and our blessing of peace. This could be a great test for yourself to know if you have actually forgiven. God is a righteous and holy judge. His timing is perfect and we can rest on God's promise that He will defend us. It is the Lord's desire that in so far as it is possible with us that we live at peace with all people, even those individuals who have scarred our lives.

***Thirdly we need to seek forgiveness for ourselves for wanting to repay evil for evil. It is natural for us to wish to hurt those that hurt us. But it is the Lord's desire that we follow His commands to leave vengeance to him. Therefore we can rest assured that if we release our desire to repay someone for a wrong we suffered God will take care of the matter in His timing.

We don't have to live as a Christian for years before we grasp the reality of forgiveness. So whether we have been saved just a few minutes or for several years the power to assist us in forgiving has been placed in us. As we release and forgive the light of Jesus that God placed inside our diamond begins to shine with the hope and mercy we seek. God will actually handle the problems of our past for us and allow us to focus on forgiveness. Forgiveness begins the process of healing the hurts of the past and not allowing them to depress the progress we are making. Once we learn to allow the Holy Spirit and the Word of God to exchange the hurt and frustration of the past with grace and peace, we can begin to understand what role forgiveness has in our lives. As we start to trust in what the Bible says about God's nature and how He is able to bind up our broken heart we can begin to forgive those that treated us unjustly. We eventually begin to realize that even in the middle of our pain God is in charge. He is a righteous judge and will be faithful to defend us.

The emotional pain of past abuses needs to be exchanged with the healing that forgiveness brings. Will we be able to forgive and forget? Forgiveness will alter our attitude toward the abuser, but the memory of what happened will not usually disappear. Which of us with a natural healthy mind can forget all that happened to us in the past? Even with a one hundred percent wonderful supportive upbringing, there is still much hurtfulness we have to face in the world. There are some past events that seem to cling to us more than others and thus are harder to forget. Our minds are a remembering machine and some things we can't ever seem to forget. But even with those memories our hearts can be at peace, which will cause our emotions to settle down. We may forgive someone and be able to look into the eyes of the abuser with a pure heart, but in those same eyes we remember in vivid detail what they said or did to us. So while complete forgetting is not always possible, a heart filled with peace and release is very possible.

Also within forgiveness is the wisdom not to allow those hurtful things to happen again. Therefore in some cases it is best not to forget. Here is a real life example: At a conference in Winston-Salam, NC, I heard a well know Christian speak of the sexual abuse she endured as a child from her father. As an adult she forgave him and tried to forget her past. Then she attempted to trust this man with her daughters, later to realize that he was now scheming to abuse her children. Was she wrong in trying to forget? No. But at the same time she could not rely on this man who created so much suffering to change. Abuses that cause real harm or danger to another person should be remembered for safety's sake. No need to give the schemer more victims. Remember that just because we did right in forgiving does not mean the abuser suddenly became a trustworthy person. The people who abused us will not necessarily have any remorse for what happened and we may never receive an apology.

After my damaged childhood, my desire was to rear my son in a loving home. Thankfully I can only recall twice that I disciplined him out of anger. But still I made many mistakes and bad choices. I could blame those poor choices on my troubled childhood because of the physical, verbal, sexual and mental abuse I suffered at the hands of adults and peers. Instead I learned through many mistakes that the choices I made could not be covered with the blame game of, "Oh look at what happened to me." No, I had to choose to see my past for what it has become. The Lord has shown me that through the act of forgiveness the past and its troubles do not define my future. Even with the memories of a damaged childhood I can still have a peaceful life. So happily now my past has become a reason to reach out and to help someone else.

Forgiveness allows us to release the accused and the pain thus finding freedom from the agony of the past. This usually is a progression not an event. It often doesn't happen overnight, and many issues must be carefully considered and worked through. Just like the Dusty Diamond has many facets that need to be cleaned and polished, I had to work through so many issues just to get healthy enough to say I forgive those that wronged me. Forgiveness is a daily process and must be considered carefully and honestly. The healing will never come from halfhearted attempts to forgive. Forgiveness with its release has to become as strong as the memory to really be lasting and peaceful.

It is possible to forgive at a distance and in some cases may even be the only solution, for instance in the situation where the person has already died. There also may be real danger in confronting the abuser face to face. There is safety in dealing with those memories just between you and the Lord. Forgiveness is an act of the will, your will, not the person that hurt you. So it is possible to forgive someone without a face to face meeting. Ask the Holy Spirit to enable you to fully give these people and circumstances over to God. God is totally trustworthy and will allow us to work through the difficulty of forgiving others. As long as you have a death grip on the painful memories forgiveness will not become a reality. With the assistance of the Holy Spirit, obedience to the Word of God and much prayer we can begin to see a difference in how we look at those troubles of the past. It would be best to let go and allow the Lord to take over. He will give the peace you truly seek. Let His hand take care of everything.

So how are we to know when we have forgiven someone? We will experience a change in our heart toward the person. There was someone in my childhood that I greatly admired who violated my trust several times. When the abuse happened I was made to feel responsible for being in the wrong place at the wrong time. During the abusive years as a child and teen I had no one I could confide in about this problem because I felt it was entirely my fault. For years I suffered in silence because of this false sense of responsibly for what this adult had done to abuse me. This pain haunted me until

I accepted Christ as my savior in my late 30's. I cannot tell you the day or hour, but after much prayer and many tears I was able to think of that person with care and compassion. This was an ongoing process and the act of forgiveness wasn't complete the first few times I prayed, mainly because I was unwilling to release the grip of the memory of what had happened. Only after the Holy Spirit and the Word of God revealed the sin of bitterness I was storing up in my heart and mind, did forgiveness begin to replace the pain with a spirit of kindness. I was finally able to be in the presence of that person without feeling hatred. This was a huge difference. I was a bit skeptical at first because this loathing had been such a large part of my life up until that point. How all this pent up disgust could be replaced with kindness seemed impossible to me. This person had certainly not been kind to me. Does this forgiveness mean I trust to be alone with the past abuser? Certainly not! The memory of what happened did not disappear but I had finally been released of its grip on my heart. It was only when I was able to think of this person with kindness and with a release from God that I truly experienced what forgiveness was all about.

> *This righteousness from God comes through faith in Jesus Christ to all who believe. There is no difference 23) for all have sinned and fall short of the glory of God, 24) and are justified freely by His grace through redemption that came by Christ Jesus. Romans 3:22-24 NIV*

By studying the Bible and the life of Jesus we will understand how to live as a Christian. Jesus Christ who is the only way to God the Father and the Holy Spirit is the perfect example of how to forgive. By following Jesus' example we can begin to understand how to approach the act of forgiveness with confidence. As we learn and practice forgiveness we also learn the way to live in a more fulfilling, peaceful future. When we take small steps to be obedient to the Word of God our heart and mind will begin to feel the effects. Those facets of the Dusty Diamond that were covered in the dust of an unforgiving spirit will begin to glow with the light of Jesus. As one facet clears, it spurs on the desire to experience others shining brighter. Forgiveness can begin a freeing result of releasing all those past hurts and disappointments. As this happens we will desire to forgive even more, because we are actually able to feel the difference. God will bless our efforts as we take those small steps to forgive those in our past that caused us so much pain. So to make the Dusty Diamond shine we need to forgive others, and give the Holy Spirit and the Word of God the opportunity to do His work in our lives.

Forgiveness Q&A:

#1.What is forgiveness?

_____

_____

Romans 3:22-24

#2. Who needs to forgive?

_____

_____

Matthew 6:14-15

#3. Why should we have a forgiving heart?

_____

_____

Mark 11:25

#4. What are some of the benefits of forgiveness?

_____

_____

Proverbs 15:30

#5. What are the steps to forgiving someone?

_____

_____

2 Corinthians 2:10-11

#6. Are you ready to let go of the hurt?

_____

_____

Colossians 3:13

#7. Who will help you learn to forgive?

_____

_____

John 14:15-17

"For God, who said, "Let light shine out of darkness, made his light shine in our hearts to give us the light of the knowledge of God's glory displayed in the face of Christ. 7) But we have this <u>treasure in jars of clay</u> to show that this all-surpassing power is from God and not from us. 2 Corinthians 4:6-7 NIV

CHAPTER 4

A Cracked Pot

Yet you, Lord, are our Father. We are the clay, you
are the potter; we are all the work of your hand.
Isaiah 64:8 NIV

We are considered the clay in God's hands that he has shaped into the vessel he desires. God has formed and gifted each person with talents and abilities to carry out the tasks He has assigned. All of this happened before we were ever born, and we were not given a choice as to what kind of vessel would be fashioned. We can develop the gifts that God has given us by understanding what those gifts are and how to operate in them. Because God is the potter and we are the clay, we must bend to His desire and accept the treasure He has placed in us. This treasure in our jar of clay is the light of Jesus that is contained in our Dusty Diamond which was covered in an earlier chapter. This diamond is housed inside the clay vessel which is our body.

"We now have this light shining in our hearts, but
we ourselves are like fragile clay jars containing
this great treasure. This makes it clear that our
great power is from God, not from ourselves." 2
Corinthians 4:7 NLT

God has placed His great treasure of the light of Jesus in our Dusty Diamond that now resides in our fragile clay jar which is our body. Our body is the clay form that has been fashioned as part of the three divisions that make up our being. First there is the body, which the Bible sometimes refers to as the flesh. This is our outward appearance and the way we interact with the world around us. Second there is the soul. The soul is made up of at least three more partitions, the mind, the will and the emotions. Our mind which contains our intellect controls how we think and what we remember. The will is that strong desire that causes us to achieve the tasks before us. The emotions are how we react or respond to what is happening to, or around us. The emotions can be easily influenced in either a negative or positive way. Often if we are not careful we can allow negative emotions to control our will and mind, which in turn attempts to govern our flesh. When passions are allowed to be displayed in a negative way this action can set about a chain of events that can quickly get out of control, and can be very hurtful. We need to learn to respond to life events in a more positive way which will bring all the components of our personhood into harmony. Third is the spirit that is the treasure in our innermost being. This is where the Dusty Diamond resides. The spirit encompasses the conscience and is often implied in Christian circles as the heart. The Holy Spirit operates out of our spirit and often uses the conscience to gain our attention. Even with the many layers of the outward appearance and innermost being that make up our personally we can respond from the treasure God has placed in us.

> *"And this is my prayer: that your love may abound more and more in knowledge and depth of insight, 10) so that you may be able to discern what is best and may be pure and blameless until the day of Christ" Philippians 1:9-10 NIV*

As our knowledge and depth of insight increase we can begin to discern what we must release and forgive. God uses the circumstances in our lives to show us how to live in victory. As we begin to release the past sins and hurts over to God we become that Cracked Pot that shows the light of Jesus to the world. When we read the Bible we see there are Cracked Pots from cover to cover. Jesus Christ was the only human to live a perfect life. The rest of us are damaged and cracked by the sin in our lives. Jesus paid for our sins on the cross even though he was without sin. Jesus and the Word of God is the answer to the pain and sorrow in our past. The cares of this life and memories of our past cause cracks or wounds to be formed around our hearts and minds. These cracks which can be painful in different degrees can also be useful in allowing the light of Jesus to shine from our innermost being. We are learning to find that answer in the act of forgiveness. In the forgiveness chapter we learned about our own responsibility to forgive others. By obeying this clear command from the Word of God to forgive, the painful past we have endured becomes a window of blessing.

So how can all the scars from the past be of any benefit to another person? The fact is much good can be achieved through a potshard or a Cracked Pot. Look into the eyes of someone who has been delivered from the same situation we are experiencing. Listen to them testify about how the Lord has delivered them. These people have been there and come out the other side, wounds and all. These people are far more able to reach others than the type of individual who has not had the same struggle. A very true statement is, "There is no testimony without a test". We must endure many tests in life as children and as adults. These tests will develop scars and cracks in our lives which can be replaced with healing and light.

The Holy Spirit uses the Word of God to exchange the hurtfulness of the past with a more peaceful future. The people in our lives will witness a complete transformation in our attitude and reaction to life events. Our speech and countenance will change.

Kindness will replace the bitterness and harshness in our tone when we greet others. Instead of searching for fault all around us, we begin to find a reason to lift someone up. We will no longer desire to tear people down. We can then become a strong advocate to the power of the gospel and how the truth within the Word of God enriched our outlook on life. This adjustment in our life style from scars and cracks to peace and joy will really be apparent to our friends and family.

As we experience the healing that forgiveness brings, we begin to display the light of Jesus to the world through our Cracked Pot. We can look at the people around us with fresher eyes; see beyond our little closed sphere to people in real need. For instance that loud, filthy mouthed person that works across the room from us may turn out to be the very one who is searching for the light we now carry. Our response can really get the attention of our neighbors because they are searching for the truth too.

That immense amount of heartache we have endured in the past can be turned into an important testimony. Why let the past hurt overtake the joy we are now experiencing? We can allow the Lord to replace what we thought was a wasted part of life and make it available to others who can glean from our understanding. In this way the past does not have to be a dreaded subject. Thankfully there is really no need for explicit details to get the point across. A willingness to share the good news of what God has done for us can make all the difference to a person who is suffering. People who are suffering need to know there is an answer to the pain. As we allow the Lord to redeem the time both good and bad, He will replace the hurt with healing and reward the good. So give it a chance. The only things you will lose are the heartache and bitterness you have been trying to carry. The future will suddenly look bright, filled with hope and faith knowing that God is on your side. Jesus will become that light inside your Cracked Pot that others will see and desire.

*"Trust in the L*ORD *with all your heart and lean not on your own understanding; 6) in all your ways submit to him, and he will make your paths straight." Proverbs 3:5-6 NIV*

In the past I tried to make myself better by trusting in my limited knowledge of the Bible. At that time I had no understanding that a full hearted relationship with the Lord was the answer. Attempts at human relationships in my past were only painful and disappointing. So I became a loner, didn't want or need any help. During that time church was not an option. I thought my simple knowledge of God's Word was enough. My goal during that time was to bring the world into the reality that Jesus was Savior. My intentions may have been sound, but my knowledge was weak and I was functioning with only the pain of the past. Because of this misguided try at evangelism the fall from what I thought was grace was very painful and hard. What was meant for evil, God turned to good and now I can share that experience with you and hopefully prevent anyone else from making the same mistakes. A truly Christian life will not happen without a personal relationship with God the Father. We were never meant to go it alone; we not only need the Lord, but we also need each other. Any form of religion which consists of only outward works can never replace a relationship with the Lord, or with our brothers and sisters in Christ.

"Therefore, as we have opportunity, let us do good to all people, especially to those who belong to the family of believers." Galatians 6:10 NIV

If we are waiting for perfection in others, it will be a very long wait. We are all Cracked Pots. Jesus was the only one to live a perfect life, so don't expect another human to always have our best interest at heart. We all make many mistakes. We all have a past and most often it is filled with memories we would rather forget.

Even though life is often filled with pain and disappointment, as Christians we can trust that God is in control and is ordering our steps. We can rely on the truth that the Lord is turning all things together for our good.

As a Cracked Pot I have many reasons to be thankful for what the Lord has done for me. My life has been completely turned around. The best of living comes from a partnership with God the Father, Jesus Christ his son, and the Holy Spirit. God's leadership can be trusted. He always has our best in mind. So the Cracked Pot title can be worn as a badge of knowledge and respect.

We know the Lord God Almighty has shown his love for us and is turning our past despair into our future destiny full of hope and peace. Through the healing of past hurts we are becoming a witness for His glory and honor. Take courage and stand firm. Allow the Holy Spirit and the Word of God to replace those past memories of pain and disappointment with a bright, fruitful future. Take what God is offering us and use it for good. He is more than willing to bless our efforts, and each day that Dusty Diamond will shine even brighter through our Cracked Pot.

A Cracked Pot Q&A:

#1.Who is the clay and why?

_____

_____

Isaiah 64:8

#2. Who is the potter?

_____

_____

Isaiah 64:8

#3. How is a cracked pot used to help others?

_____

_____

2 Corinthians 4:7

#4. How are we as Christians supposed to treat others?

_____

_____

Galatians 6:10 NIV

#5. What are the parts of our being?

_____

_____

2 Corinthians 4:7 NLT

"But who can discern their own errors? Forgive my <u>hidden faults</u>. 13) Keep your servant also from willful sins; may they not rule over me. Then I will be blameless, innocent of great transgression. 14) May these words of my month and this meditation of my heart be pleasing in your sight, LORD, my Rock and my Redeemer." Psalm 19:12-14 NIV

CHAPTER 5

Hidden Places

> *"Nothing in all creation is hidden from God's sight.*
> *Everything is uncovered and laid bare before*
> *the eyes of him to whom we must give account."*
> *Hebrews 4:13 NIV*

In earlier chapters the discussion was on the act of releasing the past and its troubles that were caused by other people. When we take stock of our own lives, we are reminded of the mistakes we have also made. We all have sinned in one way or another, so we need to confess our own faults and allow the Word of God and the Holy Spirit to replace them with the light of Jesus. We need to be forgiven as well to as offer forgiveness.

So now is the time to take a closer survey at the dark spots on the diamond, the ones on the bottom left just out of sight. These concealed areas might be hidden from view, but not from our mind. Those Hidden Places need to be confessed and removed so the light from our Dusty Diamond can shine even brighter.

> *"Ask and it will be given to you; seek and you will*
> *find; knock and the door will be opened to you.*
> *8) For everyone who asks receives; the one who*
> *seeks finds; and the one who knocks, the door will*
> *be opened" Matthew 7:7-8 NIV*

The light of Jesus that we now carry will expose those Hidden Places. At first it may be embarrassing to allow Jesus to see them, but he knows about them anyway. Those Hidden Places can be revealed in our private prayer time with the Lord. This scripture instructs us to call upon the Lord for our needs. Ask the Lord for help with our sin issues and He will provide the answer. Seek the Lord and we will find Him. He is always available to answer our prayers. Knock at the door as many times as is needed to receive the answer and it will be opened for us. God always hears us when we pray, which is just a conversation with Him. We can talk to Him about anything, even about our Hidden Places. God knows about them anyway so why not just get it out in the open and deal with the sin. So when we ask we can receive, when we seek we will find and when we knock the door will be opened for us.

> *"Watch and pray so that you will not fall into temptation. The spirit is willing, but the flesh is weak." Mark 14:38 NIV*

It is beneficial for us to get old sinful ways out in the open and pray to God for forgiveness. If we need to clear our hearts by repeating our confession of sin, God is willing to allow us the time to truly let go of those sins that are trying to control our lives. Remember the spirit is willing but the body is weak. It is God's desire that we would hate the sin in our own lives. Those Hidden Places need to be exposed with the light of Jesus. With the love, mercy and grace God is willing to give us we can move forward, release those Hidden Places and receive forgiveness from the past.

When we recall the distant or recent past is there a dark sin that lingers in our minds? We convince ourselves that these little indulgences are a release from the pent up stress of our day. We believe that what we do in secret will never hurt anyone else. Yet we know that this sin is taking over our lives and will eventually be found out by those closest to us. This sinful habit can be so natural that it seems impossible to break its control over our lives. Knowing this sin is something we really would rather not repeat causes an ongoing struggle to break free of its control on our life. But this hidden sin's grip is so very strong. We can't see how to ever break free. This sin in our Hidden Place is a very powerful temptation that Satan uses to pull us back into those old bad habits. When we study the Bible we find out how God feels about all sin. Then we must face the truth that this sinful lifestyle is putting up a barrier between us and God. That sinful behavior needs to be confessed and removed.

"It is for freedom that Christ has set us free. Stand firm, then, and do not let yourselves be burdened again by a yoke of slavery. Galatians 5:1 NIV

As a personal example in my past I had a sinful habit that was one of my Hidden sins. Even as an unsaved person I knew it was wrong. But I just couldn't seem to stop something I had been doing for as long as I could remember. Still I was agreeing with God that this was a sin, but because I was so wrapped up in the memory of this sin I had no answer as to how I was ever going to stop. This habit was so natural to me that I knew there had to be a power greater than my will to cause this sin to stop controlling me. It was going to take the strength of the Lord to break the grip of this bad habit and really release me from this sin. After reading in the Bible and finding out how God feels about sin it I knew it needed to be dealt with. One day as a young Christian after giving in to the old temptation again, the personal shame was overwhelming. Instantly I realized to gain freedom from this habit I had to be willing to never do it again. God was willing to take it from me only if I would surrender myself and the sin to Him. This decision became the turning point. I was broken at last and laid face down on the floor crying out to God for help. Through many tears I confessed how terrible this sin was and how sorry I was for all the times I had committed this sin. I also acknowledged I was out of control and could not stop by myself.

The desire to stop had finally become stronger than the foothold this sin had in my life. From that moment on I have not committed that sin again. PRAISE the LORD! That Hidden Place of my diamond was free of the dark ugly sin that tried to cloud it over. If ever I felt the temptation to continue with that sin, I recalled what the Lord did for me that day.

The release from that personal Hidden sin did not occur the first time I prayed. I was too wrapped up in my selfish desires and really didn't want to stop. It is not unusual to take many steps to truly gain freedom from the past and its desire to chain us down. But the old life style with all the bad memories and sin can be replaced with the forgiveness and the light of Christ. Obedience to the Word of God will exchange those bad habits with a growing desire to be more like Jesus. As we pray for assistance the Lord hears our prayers and sees that we are serious about our heart cry to be free of these sins. Prayer allows us to be sensitive to the Holy Spirit who is knowledgeable of our everyday struggles and instructs us with the Word of God. God will always bless our desire to be more like Jesus.

> *"For I know the plans I have for you," declares the LORD, "plans to prosper you and not to harm you, plans to give you hope and a future 12) Then you will call on me and come and pray to me, and I will listen to you. 13) You will seek me and find me when you seek me with all your heart. Jeremiah 29:11-13 NIV*

We should not choose to sin over being free of those things that try to pull us back into the darkness. We certainly cannot be released from a bad habit we insist on hanging onto. Even though not a hidden sin I had a bad habit that was attempting to return. As a personal example I had a habit of smoking cigarettes from the time I was old enough to buy them. For many years I made an attempt to quit smoking, only to return to the addiction again. In

1988 I made the difficult but necessary decision to stop throwing away my hard earned money on the ever increasing cost of these cancer sticks. So I struggled to quit. This took several months to accomplish, and I had not smoked for over ten years. Then in 1999 out of nowhere came this sudden urge for a cigarette. I tried for over six months to fight the craving. The constant desire for a cigarette was so strong I knew that this bad habit was trying to return. How can I buy and smoke cigarettes again after quitting so many years ago? Smoking was something that is not easily hidden especially to a person who doesn't smoke. But the desire to begin smoking again was a temptation that became a Hidden Place in my life, because I had not shared this old desire with anyone. I was so ashamed to admit that there was a spiritual battle going on over something like cigarettes. One day while visiting my sister I gave into the temptation and smoked one of her off brand cigarettes. There was no physical effect from smoking that one cigarette. I cried all the way home; I really didn't want to start smoking again. However several days later I gave into temptation again with the brand I was using when I had quit ten years before. This time I got very sick, coughing and gagging and crying all the while. The difference was that these were tears of joy. I began to shout and praise the Lord for utterly delivering me from this bondage. It took the power of the Lord to bring about total deliverance from this old habit. This was definitely a physical and spiritual battle for me and a struggle I could not overcome alone. The Lord is so very good, and will do what it takes to bring us into His will. Since that time the temptation left me and has not been a problem.

It really doesn't matter what your problem is with a Hidden sin. Only you and the Lord will know about those Hidden Places, and He can be totally trusted. The Lord is strong and loving enough to help. If you really want to be free of a bad habit take it to the Lord. This is an undertaking that we can't do alone. The Holy Spirit will bring us the wisdom to receive from the Word of God. Obedience to what the Bible says will bring the freedom we are seeking from the burden of those dark sins. It may only be one thing or many but take it one step at a time. Don't be discouraged if the sin is still there after the first time you ask. Some habits take extended periods of time to break. Others take hardly any effort or time at all. Have faith that God will do what he promised, and stand firm in the truth that we don't have to live under the burden of sin any longer.

The Holy Spirit and the Word of God was given to us to help us be successful. Those hidden faults are making our lives miserable. We must embrace the truth in the Bible and seek forgiveness and cleansing. Another major reason to deal with these sins is the sowing and reaping principle.

> *"Do not be deceived: God cannot be mocked. A man reaps what he sows. 8) Whoever sows to please their flesh, from the flesh will reap destruction; whoever sows to please the Spirit will reap eternal life. 9) Let us not become weary in doing good, for at the proper time we will reap a harvest if we do not give up." Galatians 6:7-9 NIV*

The sowing and reaping principle is a universal truth. A seed that is sown in the ground will become a plant of the same kind. In the same way the acts of our lives affect our future. A good act brings a good harvest; a sinful act brings a sinful harvest. The sowing and reaping principle has always been a truth in our lives even before we received Jesus as Savior. As Christians we still have a harvest of either good or bad seed from our past. Salvation does not stop the reaping from seeds sown in a sinful past. It does mean that the Holy Spirit will enable us to endure the harvest from those bad seeds with faith that God is always with us. God is so very merciful. The Lord will sometimes lessen the most difficult reaping time to enable us to see his loving plan for our lives. As we set aside the sin in our past through forgiveness we can begin to sow good seeds. Even as we reap from past sins, the good we are now doing will begin to encourage our hearts. What are some of the good seeds we can start sowing? For instance be kind when we would otherwise be unkind. Give instead of expecting to get all the time. Share with those in need as we are able. Follow the Holy Spirit's lead. He is waiting to help us. The sowing and reaping principle can become a joy when we sow those good seeds and receive the good harvest.

Never allow Hidden sin to overtake the good God is placing in your life. A relationship with the Lord is much more important than anything else. Those Hidden Places we are guarding are not only dark sin, but everyday excuses and reasons we use to go it alone without Christ. Mistakes will be made but don't file them under the Hidden Places. Admit where the error occurred and take it to the Lord in prayer. Allow the Lord to remove those sins and replace them with the light of Jesus. When we are ready the Lord will cleanse us from those sinful habits and clear our heart of those Hidden Places. Then our Dusty Diamond will shine even brighter.

Hidden Places Q&A:

#1.Where is your Hidden Place?

_____

_____

Isaiah 59:1-2 NIV

#2. Why do we try to hide sin?

_____

_____

Psalm 19: 12-13 NIV

#3. Can we have victory over sin?

_____

_____

Galatians 5:1 NIV

#4. What has God offered us?

_____

_____

Jeremiah 29:11-13 NIV

#5. What is the sowing and reaping principle?

_____

_____

Galatians 6:7-9 NIV

"When pride comes, then comes disgrace, but with humility comes wisdom." Proverbs 11:2 NIV

CHAPTER 6

Pride & Self-Doubt

"First pride, then the crash, the bigger the ego, the harder the fall." Proverbs 16:18 The Message Bible

Pride is a definite problem in everyone's life. If we take this issue even back to before the creation of the earth, the sin of pride split heaven, caused Satan and a third of the angels to fall from the presence of God and later was responsible for the sin of Adam and Eve. Pride is the problem that began the principle of sin that we all have inherited. The dictionary defines pride as haughty behavior. A biblical dictionary defines haughty as showing oneself above others. It matters not which definition we care to use, pride is a problem. God's word has much to say about the sin of pride in scriptures like in Proverbs 3:34 where his Word tells us that "He mocks the proud and shows favor to the humble." He says basically the same thing in James 4:4 and 1 Peter 5:5 NIV. Because of all the past problems caused by pride this haughtiness should be heeded and avoided if we are striving for God's best.

> *20) He went on: "What comes out of a man is what makes him unclean. 21) For from within, out of men's hearts, come evil thoughts, sexual immorality, theft, murder, adultery, 22)greed, malice, deceit, lewdness, envy, slander, arrogance*

> **and folly. 23) All these evils come from inside and make a man "unclean" Mark 7:20-23 NIV**

Think back to before you ever accepted Jesus as your Savior. What was the prideful driving force that caused you to get through the day? Was it hate, fear, rage, violence, slander, back stabbing, or self-indulgence and other such responses? Or was it shyness around people, being fearful about speaking, being withdrawn to the degree of isolating yourself from others? In our pain we would either lash out in anger or withdraw in silence while inside we may have been too upset to speak. In the quest to gain acceptance we would react in a negative way to each and every person and thing seemingly standing in our way. All the while thinking as the world does that we were grabbing and growling our way to the top. In either case be it loud or silent our actions speak louder than our words proving that we are in pain. This is how we use to live and because of all this pent up prideful sin we had no tranquility. In reality these kinds of behavior is an outward demonstration of what is on the inside, a prideful spirit full of death and misery. Whatever is in the heart will come out for us and the world to see. The pride in our life such as conceit, violence or being overly shy doesn't have to control us any longer.

Pride is an issue that we need to recognize in our own lives no matter what form it takes. This most troubling rebellion of pride can be one of the hardest to spot in oneself, and very easy to assume in others.

> **"Why do you look at the speck of sawdust in your brother's eye and pay no attention to the plank in your own eye? 4) How can you say to your brother, 'Let me take the speck out of your eye' when all the time there is a plank in your own eye?" Matthew 7:3-4 NIV**

A judgmental spirit of pride is so very easy to exercise. How easy it is to allow pride to drive a wedge of mistrust between ourselves and others. It is simple to point to someone else and discuss his shortcomings instead of examining the mistakes we make ourselves. We should understand that everyone has missteps, and we as Christians are all growing in our relationship with the Lord and each other. By growing and learning to show patience and love for others we learn how to be more forgiving of the mistakes we all make. We don't have to have been born with a silver spoon to inherit a problem with conceit. A homeless person living on the street with only two dollars to his name can have a dilemma with vanity. By the same truth the common person who isn't wealthy or living on the streets can also have a real problem with pride. We all struggle with arrogance and a feeling of pride in one form or another. So now is the question, "How do we deal with this feeling of superiority, and consider others better than ourselves?"

> *"In your relationships with one another, have the same mindset as Christ Jesus: 6) Who, being in very nature God, did not consider equality with God something to be used to his own advantage; 7) rather, he made himself nothing by taking the very nature of a servant, being made in human likeness. 8) And being found in appearance as a man, he humbled himself by being obedient to death-even death on a cross! 9) Therefore God exalted him to the highest place and gave him the name that is above every name, 10) that at the name of Jesus every knee should bow, in heaven and on earth and under the earth, 11) and every tongue acknowledge that Jesus Christ is Lord, to the glory of God the Father. Philippians 2:5-11 NIV*

Jesus is our supreme example of how to be humble. He became a man to show us how to be a servant and was fully obedient to the will of God, even though he is equal to God. He was sinless, but was willing to take the full weight of sin on the cross in our place. He exchanged the glory of heaven for the cruelest of deaths, the death on a cross. This was the greatest example of humility. This humble Christ is the one who lives in us and wants to work His humility in us. Servant hood can cure the haughtiness creeping up in our lives. Wait, here is another trap! Even doing for others can cause pride to raise its ugly head. We can become puffed up with our own self-importance. The temptation to become proud of oneself and accomplishments made can be so over powering. Obedience to the principles in the Word of God will help cure this problem with ever growing egotism. If we study the life of Jesus we can better understand how to be humble. As we learn to submit ourselves to the Christ within, we find we are changing and growing deeper in humility.

> *"Be completely humble and gentle; be patient, bearing with one another in love. 3) Make every effort to keep the unity of the Spirit through the bond of peace. Ephesians 4:2-3 NIV*

One of the triggers that will often cause pride to well up in us is the spirit of jealously. Jealously can be very destructive and at its root is the spirit of pride. If we are dominated by a spirit of jealously there is no true contentment. We become bound in a desire to control everything that goes on around us. As we see others promoted before us, or see them come into a blessing we have sought and prayed for, then a sense of entitlement can begin and when left unresolved can soon turn into a prideful jealous spirit. An important part of the cure for this resentment is to be truly thankful for what God has done for us and also be thankful for what blessings have been given to someone else. After all someone else being blessed does not hurt me or keep me from be blessed. We can always find something to rejoice over which will lessen the spirit of pride and jealously in our lives.

There is a difference between being happy and being prideful. There are some things we can be pleased with without trying to make ourselves better than others. For instance; I am very gratified to be a Christian. Just to know God loves me for me and that He has given His Holy Word, Jesus and the Holy Spirit for me is beyond human comprehension. I'm honored to be a member of my family because they are a huge part of me, the good and the bad. My Christian friends give me a sense of elation. I look at their lives and am motivated by how they stand for the gospel in spite of all the troubles they endure. The work I do and how I do it is a source of being content, not because I am better than my co-workers, but that the work of my hands mean something to the Lord and to me.

Another part of the cure for the pride issues is that we have never nor will ever live this life alone. God is always with us, even in the times we act like the devil. He has given us a free will to decide what we are going to do with this time He has granted to us. Within the exchanging work of the Holy Spirit, we can see the difference it makes to live life and make choices God's way. This is not easy and we are not mindless puppets. If we were not so stubborn and prideful, we would be obedient to God's Word and allow the Holy Spirit to show us how to live in humility each and every day. It is a fact that we can't even breathe without God's permission. We are only one heartbeat from heaven. Just like the return of Jesus, only God knows when our last day on earth will be. As we realize our complete dependence upon God our attitudes become more humble and less apt to be prideful. As we attempt to be the type of person who uses his gifts to help others know the truth, we can put pride in its place and decide to live in freedom. We are not in charge, so let God lead the way and begin to see what a victorious life looks and feels like.

Of all the subjects in this study this issue of pride can be the hardest to deal with for us. As long as we are on this side of heaven pride will be an issue. Even with all the effort to become humble and be a servant, the pride problem is still under the surface for many of us. So it is best for us to recognize it before it swallows up our very lives. If you were told that the Christian life was easy, I am here to tell you it is not. It is for certain that dealing with pride is one of the things that make the Christian life difficult. Each day we must decide which route we are going to walk on, the pride path or the servant path. The sooner we can know when the wrong course is being taken the better. It is very easy for us to fall into the trap of pride. Pride is often deceitful and hides from us. We simply do not recognize it. Our human solution to everyday issues with pride is only on the surface. If we try doing all this changing on our own, in the end we will fail. We cannot effect change within our hearts without being in partnership with the Holy Spirit and obedience to God's Word. The Lord will assist us in this vital exchange from pride to humility so we can run this race successfully.

> *"Good and upright is the LORD; therefore he instructs sinners in his ways. 9) He guides the humble in what is right and teaches them his way."*
> *Psalm 25:8-9 NIV*

As we seek to grow in our faith we will need other Christians around us to help us grow in spirit and truth. We can allow the Holy Spirit to guide us to others who can help us to become mature in the faith. Life itself is not easy and there could be struggles with issues that may try to divide a new relationship even if this relationship is between Christians. We know that we were not born with a humble spirit. Humility is something that has to be discovered in Christ. We need to allow the exchange of our pride for Christ's humility. There are no perfect people here, so we must go into a relationship with another person with a humble spirit. We all make mistakes and must forgive as well as be forgiven. We can get the feeling that we are being humble, but that impression could be completely wrong.

It takes much prayer and reading the Bible to understand how this Christian life is supposed to be lived.

Self-doubt is another side of the pride issue. This one is way down on the bottom of our Dusty Diamond. Because we have a habit of hiding it so well others cannot detect that self-doubt is present in our lives. In our desire to appear in control we could very well be hiding a problem with self-doubt. No one has all the correct answers all the time. Still we should not depend on just our limited ability to navigate the issues facing us each day. As we read the Word of God we will understand that He is more than able to communicate with us. Self-doubt actually hit me hard on the way to work this morning. These words came so plainly to my mind. "What makes you think YOU have been called by the Lord to do anything to impact someone else's life?" At that same time, while driving and listening to the Christian radio station, a song was played that told me the answer. Now I have been assured by the Lord that what I am doing is right, and not to listen to self-doubt. There will always be someone who could do a task better. As said in an earlier chapter I don't have all the answers. But what I do have I must share in a way that can possibly make a difference to somebody. The sense of pride and self-doubt will try to stop our growth in the Lord, but we must not allow these sins to keep us bound.

> *"Because the Sovereign LORD helps me, I will not be disgraced. Therefore have I set my face like flint, and know I will not be put to shame." Isaiah 50:7 NIV*

Certainly the problem of self-doubt has killed many a dream over the ages. In my own life I have heard stories of regret from friends and family that did not overcome self-doubt. Fear of the future and what others thought caused them to withdraw from what God was clearly calling them to accomplish. As I take stock of my own life there is more past than future. There are issues I have lived through that may help someone else see the light of Jesus and how He has changed my life. Now is the time to break out of the cycle of self-doubt and put on humility. Self-doubt can weight a body down and lead directly to a state of depression. This becomes a deep dark hole that we may never be able to shake. The Lord is trying to say to us that He has this life we live in His hands, and we must trust Him. He knows the end from the beginning and is more than able to accomplish His will in our lives, even when we don't understand. At times we may have to repeat to our own souls not to worry that God is loving and merciful, even when things look bleak. We must begin to trust what the Word of God and Holy Spirit is doing in us, and that work of cleansing and exchange can be painful at times. We are to just hold on, stand firm, set our faces like flint and the Lord will take us through to the end.

Pride & Self-Doubt Q&A:

#1.Where does pride come from?

_____

_____

Isaiah 14:11-15

#2. Why is it easy to be depressed?

_____

_____

Psalm 109:22

#3. How does God feel about pride?

_____

_____

Proverbs 16:5

#4. What do we see in others, but not in ourselves?

_____

_____

Matthew 7:3-4

#5. What can we do to prevent the self-doubt problem?

_____

_____

James 1:5-6

#6. How can we have victory over pride?

_____

_____

Matthew 20:26-28

#7. Will God help us with the problem of pride and self-doubt?

_____

_____

Isaiah 50:7 NIV

"When I was a child, my speech, feelings, and thinking were all those of a child; now that I am an adult, I have no more use for childish ways." 1 Corinthians 13:11 GNT

CHAPTER 7

Breaking the Cycle

"For I know the plans I have for you," declares the LORD, "plans to prosper you and not to harm you, plans to give you hope and a future." Jeremiah 29:11 NIV

Is that cycle of an unforgiving spirit causing you pain today? The past is just that, and we can never revisit there except in our own mind. Why try to change something that we experienced years ago when we had no idea what it had to do with our future? Only God has the ability to know what our future holds and how the past will affect the times to come. He knows best how to provide us with the future he has planned for us. There could be many spiritual challenges ahead. But with the Holy Spirit as our helper we can face whatever comes our way. We will experience wisdom when we follow the plan the Lord has made for our lives. The choices I made as an unsaved person 35 years ago may not have been ideal. But never the less they cannot be undone. God has blessed me in spite of the choices I made back then. As I walk in the light of forgiveness that God has granted, I am able to make choices that will produce an even better future. There are grandchildren in my life I would never want to harm by changing what happened before they were born. The choice I desire is to forgive and break the cycle of pain.

As we strive to follow the Holy Spirit's lead we can learn how to handle life's challenges in a more positive way. The struggles that we gain victory over will cause a layer of dust to fall away from our Dusty Diamond. This in turn will allow those people with whom we come in contact to see the light of Jesus that is inside our diamond. If we spend most of our day around unsaved people it becomes easy to get caught up in the attitude of these people. There are times when we must step out of our comfort zones so that the individuals around us can see how we have learned to handle everyday issues. As Christians we can become the example of how to break the cycle of distress that causes problems.

As we interact with people all day long we can practice the act of forgiveness. Sometimes it may be easier to be forgiving of a total stranger than to forgive a friend or family member because that person is not so involved in our lives. It is totally unrealistic and unfair to expect an unsaved person to respond as a Christian rather they are friend, family or stranger. What are we to do if we face the daily wickedness of an unsaved person? The stress of unprovoked anger aimed toward us can cause our witness to fade and makes this walk as a Christian even harder. The temptation to rip back at these individuals can really put any progress we were making into a tail spin. We eventually learn to restrict the urge to be out of control with stressful emotions. By showing kindness in these types of situations it is possible these people will begin to see the difference Jesus has made in our lives. As we break the cycle of disharmony for them, hopefully they will see and hear how a Christian responds to life's challenges. Even though they don't know how to forgive, they will see the results as we practice the act of forgiveness each day. We may not be perfect in these types of forgiving responses but every time we succeed it is all positive in every way.

"Anxiety weighs down the heart, but a kind word cheers it up." Proverbs 12:25 NIV

When we experience a painful problem it can never be resolved by reacting in a negative way. The cycle of trouble will always multiply trouble. Pain can only breed pain. Hurting people desire to hurt people. Sadness only communicates sadness. Our attempts to enact revenge will never be satisfied. Hateful words are usually repeated. The only way to break free of the cycle of pain is to handle troubling concerns with the assistance of the Holy Spirit. As we learn daily how to break the cycle of pain we allow the light of Jesus to shine on the problem and to show us that blessed people are a blessing to others. Love will replace hate. Joy is the substitution for sadness. Forgiveness brings about healing. Kind words will usually soothe the soul. A kind word will almost always calm the situation and turn away the wrath of another person. The only way to handle negative feedback is to apply the truth in love, understanding and a forgiving spirit.

As we have attempted to practice the act of forgiveness, there may still be lingering doubt if we have really achieved freedom from the cycle of the painful memories of the past. Without the assistance of the Holy Spirit forgiveness is not possible. Even if we have the desire to move on and face the future with a better state of mind we can't as long as we are seeking revenge. The act of not releasing the past and its troubles is a sure indication that we have not achieved full and complete forgiveness. The memory of past hurts may still be lingering in our minds. There are some things we will always remember. But our hearts can be free of the desire to repay pain for pain. That is when we know we are finally free and have broken the cycle of hurt.

Most people are alike in that we remember how we were treated by the individuals that were most important in our lives. If that treatment was negative it becomes a cycle of pain. The only way to break out of that memory is to forgive those responsible. When we break the cycle of a regretful past we will experience changes that will transform the way we deal with life and other people. When we fully forgive we will experience release from the memories that were hurtful. Once we truly experience the freedom and release forgiveness provides we will be willing to continue this act of grace and mercy. This in turn will cause the light from our Dusty Diamond to be visual for the people with whom we come in contact with to see.

> *"And he who searches our hearts knows the mind of the Spirit, because the Spirit intercedes for the saints in accordance with God's will." Romans 8:27 NIV*

As we seek to break the cycle of pain in our lives, we must let go and allow God to heal those deep hurts from our past. God cannot and will not bless sin. That negative cycle of an unforgiving heart is sin. It can't be plastered over with excuses; God looks on the heart. It matters not if the pain was five minutes ago, five years ago or 50 years ago. God has already offered us the peace that will allow us to live a more productive, joyful life. We can't blame the Lord if we hold on to the cycle of bitterness in our heart. The power to forgive has not only been demonstrated by Jesus on the cross, but that same forgiving power of Jesus has also been placed in our hearts.

> *"For our struggle is not against flesh and blood, but against the rulers, against the authorities, against the powers of this dark world and against the spiritual forces of evil in the heavenly realms" Ephesians 6:12 NIV*

The enemy of our soul would have us battling over issues that should not divide friends or coworkers. Our battle is not with people. Our battle is with the spiritual realm. Even the most hardened person on the outside was once a little child that was hurt in ways we can never understand. At times we are dealing with people who have raw emotions. Those emotions can be displayed in a number of different ways. They might use their tongues to lash out with words that burn our ears. They may become very withdrawn and quiet.

They could even react with a display such as throwing things or even causing physical harm to others and sometimes to themselves. These outward reactions could very well be a cry for help. We soon learn to pray that the Lord will give us the words to say to help break the cycle of pain. We would become even kinder toward people if we could see inside their lives to the pain they have experienced. The people that are unsaved are not the only ones with problems of the past. Christians can also have a tender spot and it only takes a very small amount of pressure to release tears or anger. It takes some individuals a long time to release and recover from past abuses. There are people who think they will never completely recover from the cycle of pain. But healing and deliverance is possible through Christ. And our response to these hurting people is important.

Another troubling topic is forgiving oneself. Is there something in the past that is haunting your thoughts? Are you wishing you could break free of the cycle of guilt that keeps returning when it is least expected? Have you searched your heart and submitted all to the Lord? Guilt could be one of those hidden places in your diamond, the hidden place only you and the Lord know about. Perhaps what is troubling you happened years ago when you were a pagan, and cared for nothing but what you thought made you feel better. Are there emotions that use to burn in your soul that would tempt you to say and to do things you would never dream of doing now that you have received salvation? We mistakenly think that the act of salvation cured all those rotten memories. Still that cycle of sin lingers in our mind, just enough to attempt to drag us off course. God has forgiven us, but he may be allowing that memory to invade our thoughts to warn us not to indulge in those old sins. It is time to choose to make a decision against the sin and to turn away from those sinful memories. If we entertain a past sin in our minds, then we refuse to accept the free gift of mercy God has provided. Remember the sowing and reaping principle? That truth applies here too, so a past sin does not have to rule over our lives.

"In the same way, count yourselves dead to sin but alive to God in Christ Jesus. 12) Therefore do not let sin reign in your mortal body so that you obey its evil desires. 13) Do not offer the parts of your body to sin, as instruments of wickedness, but rather offer yourselves to God, as those who have been brought from death to life; and offer the parts of your body to him as instruments of righteousness. 14) For sin shall not be your master, because you are not under the law, but under grace." Romans 6:11-14 NIV

Paul is talking to the Romans about the difference between the law and grace. The law was given to point us to the sin in our lives, and grace is there to remove the sin. Determine that grace is controlling the way we live now and sin has to be put under our feet. The Holy Spirit desires to make us more like Jesus, who died for all sin, past, present and future. So now we too have the capability to break the cycle of sin. It all began when we asked the Lord for forgiveness. He granted forgiveness to us and gave us the Holy Spirit as a teacher and guide. With the Holy Spirit's help we become more sensitive to those sinful things in our life that use to be second nature.

"Or didn't you realize that your body is a sacred place, the place of the Holy Spirit? Don't you see that you can't live however you please; squandering what God paid such a high price for? The physical part of you is not some piece of property belonging to the spiritual part of you. God owns the whole works. So let people see God in and through your body." 1 Corinthians 6:19-20 The Message Bible

It can be a real struggle to let go of the cycle of what was common to us. As a personal example I grew up with music all around me. My Dad played the guitar and my Grandmother Frances played the piano. I would wake up each morning to the sounds of Country music from the radio that my Mother listened to. When I became a Christian at age 36 I began listening to Christian radio. I was only listening to Christian music then as now because my life had radically changed and I needed the constant support of what I heard to edify me. At that time I was working in a factory and was permitted to bring my radio to the area to which I was assigned. This also meant everyone else had the same freedom so different musical styles were surrounding me daily. One particular day I caught myself listening closely to a song from my past. As I began to sing along with it, I felt the Holy Spirit stop me. What most people would classify as harmless was causing me severe physical withdrawal pains. The battle was so very strong that day and I remember breaking out in a cold sweat. I began to pray to the Lord for deliverance from the style of music that was causing this spiritual battle. Is listening to any musical style other than Christian songs a sin? The answer involves what message the music is sending. Listening to that style of music was wrong for me because of all those years of embracing the message in their lyrics. Some might call this desire to follow the Holy Spirit a form of restriction or legalism. But for me it is a way to break the cycle of sin and gain freedom. God created music, and all through the Bible music is used to glorify Him. Satan uses music to tempt and destroy individuals who fall victim to the lies contained within the words of a song. If we listen to any evil message long enough it will become truth to us. There is a child's song that says "Be careful little eyes what you see, be careful little ears what you hear". This is a reality in life that we do remember what we see and hear. This becomes a recorder in our brains that at times won't shut off. I had to seek forgiveness to break the cycle of a musical style that did not honor God. The experience was a real physical struggle. God was faithful as He always is, and the Holy Spirit delivered me.

At around this same time a nationally known Country music singer was coming to our little town. During a lunch break one of my co-workers asked me if I had plans to attend to this concert. I asked who this person was and all the women at the lunch table laughed at me. They could not believe I had never heard this song or the name of the person who sang it. I can still remember the look on their faces. Talk about being uncomfortable and feeling awkward, I was that day. Still I did not apologize for my lack of Country music knowledge. Sometimes other musical styles are unavoidable, but I care not to embrace the message of the worldly ideas put to music. To me this is proof that the Holy Spirit is leading my life. I can testify that my life belongs to the Lord, and this sin cannot rule over me. Maybe you have no problem listening to different forms of music; your pull may be altogether different. That is a subject you must struggle with and allow the Holy Spirit to help you overcome.

> *"The weapons we use in our fight are not the world's weapons but God's powerful weapons, which we use to destroy strongholds. We destroy false arguments; 5) we pull down every proud obstacle that is raised against the knowledge of God; we take every thought captive and make it obey Christ." 2 Corinthians 10:4-5 GNT*

Life at times can be a powerful struggle. There may be days when it feels like the struggle is too hard to endure. When we received salvation our outlook on life changed, but we still have sinful, painful past to live through. Those painful memories can easily become a cycle of sin that attempts to weigh us down. Just remember that God is truly on our side and will equip us with the tools necessary to destroy the strongholds in our lives. It is our decision to break that cycle of pain and live in the freedom offered to us by the Lord. As Christians we are in the world, but not of the world. This just means we are set apart to live a totally different life than what we did before receiving salvation. The Holy Spirit is given to us to assist us in this radical lifestyle change. He will not force us to do anything. We have a free will to choose to follow his lead. We need to determine that the hurtful cycle of the past must not rule over us any longer. Breaking the cycle of pain will remove the dust from our Dusty Diamond and bring healing and light to us and the people we meet daily.

Breaking the Cycle Q&A:

#1.How does maturity break the cycle of old sin patterns?

_____

_____

1 Corinthians 13:11 GNT

#2. What will turn away the anger from someone?

_____

_____

Proverbs 12:25 NIV

#3. How do we avoid the traps of sin?

_____

_____

Romans 6:11-14 NIV

#4. Where does God search?

_____

_____

Romans 8:27 NIV

#5. What is our struggle against?

_____

_____

Ephesians 6:12 NIV

#6. How can we have victory over sin?

_____

_____

2 Corinthians 10:4-5 GNT

#7. As a Christian what part of me belongs to God?

_____

_____

1 Corinthians 6:19-20 TMB

*"For the L*ORD *your God is the one who goes with you to fight for you against your enemies to give you victory." Deuteronomy 20:4 NIV*

Chapter 8

Living in Victory

"But thanks be to God! He gives us the victory through our Lord Jesus Christ". 1 Corinthians 15:57 NIV

Living in victory is achieved when we are in step with God's plans. How is victory defined? What exactly is the victory we are seeking? Victory for the Christian is a whole lifestyle of following the Word of God in obedience. Obedience to the Word of God is our protection from all past sin from which we have been delivered. Also obedience will determine God's will for our lives today. God has a better plan than we could ever imagine. So living in step with His will is a choice we will make to obtain the victory we seek. I have chosen to not be a victim but to live in the victory God offers.

What if the ordeal we are experiencing today seems to be impossible to live through? There are so many peaks and valleys during our lives. One day we are celebrating on the mountain top. But the very next day we are hit with a problem that is totally unexpected. These ever changing events can cause us to become easily discouraged. The past could have been very difficult, but so can the problems we are facing today. There has to be a way to gain peace in the middle of dealing with the past and present turmoil. Often it is hard to imagine that anything good can come from these hardships. Success will not come without a struggle. If we can briefly take our eyes off the problem and remember what God has done for us in the past and look to His promises for the future, He will replace the pain with peace. Our body may not be as healthy as we would like or perhaps we are still facing the mountain that will not move. But with Jesus in our hearts and guidance from the Holy Spirit, and obedience to God's Word we can stand on the truths that God reveals to us in His Word. God's promises are sure. They are yes for us in Jesus Christ. Therefore no matter what goes on around us we can still live in victory. God's gentle loving caring hand will guide us. Praise the Lord! He will not allow us to cross certain lines.

God's Word has made a huge impact on my life and I praise His name for the truth that has set me free. There has been another influence in my walk as a Christian. Those are the people I come in contact with at church. Many of these brothers and sisters in Christ have lived out love in front of me. They accepted me and all my mess when I first came to truly believe in Christ. It was their hugs and kind words that allowed me time to adjust to this brand new way of life. As I watched and listened closely I also learned to love in a way that I had never known before. These wonderful people accepted me and allowed the growth needed to learn how to live as a Christian. These church people are not perfect but their hearts are bent toward God and His Word. It is because of this history that I can testify to the goodness of the people who strive to truly follow God's commands. This history with God has given me the victory over the sin in my life. There has been a radical change in my heart and mind. Even though the memories of abuse and regret can make themselves present in my thoughts they only serve to prove the goodness of the Lord and what He has done in my life. This is how I know He has a perfect plan for our lives. I have not only read the Word of God and accepted it by faith, but I personally have experienced the reality of the Word of God. The promises that God has given in His Word have worked in my life. And these promises are available for you also as you read and follow the His Word. Are there still challenges? Yes very much so, but I know who holds the future and I can totally trust Him with my life. And so can you. We now have a relationship with the living God. That partnership allows us to leave the past behind and focus on the present and future.

"For our struggle is not against flesh and blood, but against the rulers, against the authorities, against the powers of this dark world and against the spiritual forces of evil in the heavenly realms."
Ephesians 6:12 NIV

As we struggle to get through a trial that we may be facing it is helpful to remember this scripture. Even though we may be facing a person that has or is causing us a problem our struggle is not against our neighbor, but against the evil in the heavenly realms. This is where the phrase "Love the person, hate the sin" comes into reality. We may have to step away from a possible conflict just to be able to see where the trouble has originated. Forgiveness is still the tool we need to exercise to gain the victory. This becomes a reason to rely on the Lord even more. We cannot fight the enemy of our souls alone. The victory has already been won for us because we have released the situation and person to God. Now our focus has been turned to the Lord allowing Him to calm our hearts. There will be times when anger or other negative emotions want to rise up and cause havoc. It is at times like this that the Holy Spirit gently reminds us to calm down and look at the bigger picture. Even though the person may be right before us, we need to remember that they are being influenced and oppressed by the evil surrounding them in the heavenly realms. The heavenly realm that this scripture refers to is the spiritual areas around each person. Surrounding each individual is a spirit of either good or evil. Because we have the gift of the Holy Spirit residing within us, our spirit can often identify when an evil spirit is trying to control a circumstance we may be facing. Although as a human being, we cannot expect to understand each and every circumstance completely, we know the ultimate victory is ours in Jesus Christ. The only way to handle troubling issues with our neighbor is to rely on the guidance of the Holy Spirit and the basic instruction of the scriptures that tell us how to have victory over the schemes working against us.

> *"Watch and pray so that you will not fall into temptation. The spirit is willing, but the body is weak" Matthew 26:41 NIV*

Jesus was talking to his disciples in this scripture, but it applies to our lives as well. The demonic oppression is always waiting on the outside trying to gain a foothold into our thought life. Now that we belong to the Lord this demonic oppression uses temptation to cause us to fall back into old patterns of living. If you find that your thought life is focusing on sinful behaviors don't remain there. There is danger in spending too much thought time on what has already been forgiven. Jesus has gained the victory over Satan, therefore we have also. The salvation we received is based on what Jesus did for us on the cross. But it also involves our willingness to repent and release the sinful past we were living in before we accepted Christ. Appling the knowledge to the struggles and temptations we face will cause Satan to back down as we center our attention on the mercy and grace of the Lord. We can stay strong and know that God the Father, Jesus, and the Holy Spirit are here to keep us on the correct path.

> *"And God is able to bless you abundantly, so that in all things at all times, having all that you need, you will abound in every good work." 2 Corinthians 9:8 NIV*

As long as we live in these earthly bodies there will be difficult days, and sometimes years. Even with the assistance of the Holy Spirit and the guidance from the Word of God we still have to face the world and all the traps trying to pull us back into sin. We soon learn to lean hard on the Lord who brings us through when life looks impossible. A history of bad habits and friends can drag us away from the truth. We must not allow anything or anyone to rob what God has placed in our lives. Jesus came to give us life and that much more abundantly. We need to become sensitive to what the Holy Spirit is trying to do for us. The gift of the Holy Spirit is within our Dusty Diamond that resides in our innermost being to guide us in the way of truth. God has given us a free will and that free will is a spiritual gift. With it we get to choose which direction we desire to follow. This is the reason we need the Word of God to guide us. At times the message is very clear. At other times it is difficult to experience God's leadership through all the clutter of everyday life. We get our instruction for victorious living within the pages of the Word of God. And we base our relationship with the Lord of the universe on this same Word. The victory is ours when we live in the realization that this Word is living truth. This Christian life is much more than a meaningless mindless exercise with a humanly designed idea of God.

God is so long suffering. He waits for us to come to the realization that we cannot save ourselves. He is always willing to take us in and give us His Holy Spirit. Even though we are completely unworthy, He offers us the free gift of grace. Why should He trust us with the gift of His only son Jesus and the Holy Spirit, knowing we are prone to sin? He sent His only Son for us, to die the death we deserve. Through forgiveness of sin, we are set free to live the way God intended. So how can we possibly refuse to follow His instruction to forgive others? God will never force us to do anything, but as He waits patiently for us to come around to His will for our lives. He will sometimes intervene with discipline and reaping that will help us realize the changes we need to make. As we have read in the Bible, His love, mercy, grace and protection is there for us too. In order for us to live in victory we must surrender our mind, will and emotions which control our flesh, soul and spirit, to the Lord so that the exchange from darkness to victory can begin. This life is an everyday, hour and minute walk to experience the full blessing God has stored up for us. The Lord is more than able to direct the comings and goings of our lives. But we are not mindless puppets, and He has given us a free will. Learn whatever you can to help clear up the clutter in your thought life so that you can distinguish His leadership. Making an attempt to read the Bible and pray each day will be very helpful. You will appreciate a version of the Bible you can fully understand. You may want to join a small group study in the church you attend and thus learn from those who have been doing this Christian walk longer than you have. Such fellowship helps us to learn and experience the power of a forgiving lifestyle.

Reaching out to people and showing the love of God through certain acts is a demonstration of the forgiveness in our hearts. There may be a time when that reaching out is to a group of people with whom we are not completely comfortable. And then there are times when we need to show this same love to those we are most comfortable with. There are so many avenues to reaching people and showing the love of God. They need us but at times we need them more. Their lives will cause us to break down our will and put on Jesus. In this way they may see who He really is. So strive to be that witness our unsaved friends and family look to when they need prayer or encouragement. People don't worry as much for Bible verse addresses as they do that someone is able to live them out. "They won't care what you know, until they know that you care"! Just as there are no two people exactly the same there are countless ways we can "Let our little light shine" as a testimony of the goodness God desires to pour out on all flesh. We are not all pastors or leaders in the church. So we must use the talents and gifts God gave us to help others. We can only be saved a few minutes and be able to testify to the lost people we come in contact with each day. We are all able to demonstrate the love of God to our group of friends. The people I come in contact with are totally different than your inner circle of friends. We may even go to church together or work side by side and still we know individuals that the other doesn't. So be ready in and out of season to show what the love of God looks and acts like. Each day is a new slate and an opportunity to live in a way that will show Jesus to the world. Remember that God is responsible for salvation. We just need to live that salvation out and allow our Dusty Diamond to shine with the light of Jesus in as full a measure as possible.

Living a Christian life can have its challenges. The sin principle we were born with can make life hard to understand. We need to accept the fact that Jesus forgave us on the cross and desires to live in and through us. As we begin to forgive those that have wronged us we can then start the healing process of the bad and painful memories of the past. The Holy Spirit will exchange those hurtful scars with the mercy and grace of God. As this happens we begin to see beyond the pain to a better future instead of dwelling on those hidden places from our past. The Dusty Diamond inside our soul will shine brightly as we forgive and learn to live with the memories good and bad. When we see others around us suffering, we can share what the Lord has done for us and encourage instead of tear down. We can let go of the pride in our lives and show compassion to the folks we come in contact with each day. Our lives can be a testimony of how to break the cycle of regret and shame. Our freedom can become the example of how to live in victory. In this way we can live life the way God intended. Then the light in our Dusty Diamond will draw all people to Jesus.

"May the grace of the Lord Jesus Christ, and the love of God, and the fellowship of the Holy Spirit be with you all." 2 Corinthians 13:14 NIV

Living in Victory Q&A:

#1.What did we learn about the Dusty Diamond?

_____

_____

2 Corinthians 4:6 NIV

#2. In what Condition were we all born?

_____

_____

Psalm 51:5 NIV

#3. How do we Forgive someone?

_____

_____

Romans 12:17-18 NIV

#4. How will our Cracked Pot help someone else?

_____

_____

2 Corinthians 4:6-7 NIV

#5. Where is the Hidden Place in our lives?

_____

_____

Hebrews 4:13 NIV

#6. What has the sin of Pride done to the human race?

_____

_____

Proverbs 16:18 The Message Bible

#7. How can we Break the Cycle of pain?

_____

_____

Ephesians 6:12 NIV

#8. How are we to live in Victory?

_____

_____

1 Corinthians 15:57 NIV